How to Use a Sewing Machine: Beginner Tips, Techniques, Needles, Accessories, Art, & More

By Margaret Singer

Copyright 2019
Third Edition, License Notes

Copyright Info:

Legal Info:

This author and or rights owner(s) make no claims, promises, or guarantees in regards to the accuracy, completeness, or adequacy of the contents of this book, and expressly disclaims liability for errors and omissions in the contents within. This product is for reference use only. Please consult a professional before taking action on any of the contents found within.

Preface

We want to take a moment to say thank you for purchasing our guide online. HiddenStuff Entertainment remains one of the top app and eBook publishers online. It is our commitment to bring you the most important information to enrich your life.

We sincerely hope that you find this guide useful and beneficial in your quest for betterment. We want to provide readers with knowledge and build their skills to perform at the highest levels within their topics of interest. This in turn contributes to a positive and more enjoyable experience. After all, it is our belief that things in life are to be enjoyed as much as they possibly can be.

If you are in need of additional support or resources in regards to this guide, please feel free to visit our webpage at Hiddenstuffentertainment.com

Contents

Introduction

You are very excited because of that new sewing machine. However, the major challenge is the fact that you don't understand how to make effective use of it. This isn't hard to figure out once you know the right steps to take. There is no need being worried as this tutorial will help to provide you with a walkthrough.

Alright, you have been able to buy the sewing machine that you've always dreamt of. What are the buttons as well as levers? Is there any way that you can get this thing turned on?

It is really exciting to have a sewing machine. However, such an excitement can be turned into frustration once you seem confused about the functions that various gadgets are actually meant for. The first step to solve all of such puzzles is to understand how to make use of a sewing machine. With this guide, you will definitely understand how it can be used effectively.

Using a sewing machine

First of all, note that sewing machines aren't the same. In that case, I will be doing everything I can to ensure that you have a better understanding about your machine even though it may be slightly different from what I have got here. You will get a lot of help from your user manual.

There are 2 types of sewing machines that I will be showing you today. The first one is that owned by a friend of mine named Carrie. The reason I am showing you this one is that there is a high chance of it being similar to the one you will be using at the moment. After that, we can look at the one I have.

The sewing machine of Carrie is basic Janome. I never knew she had this type of machine until I requested if I could borrow it in order to take some snapshots.

I actually love these types of machines because with them, you will always get it right. I have come to understand that Janome has a baby sister which is Kenmore. It is also highly recommended. I started by using Kenmore.

The first thing to do is locate the power cord as well as switch point (on/off).

Learning how to use a sewing machine

The foot pedal is where the power cord is attached to. Your foot will be able to reach it (the foot pedal) comfortably since it is on the floor.

There are various knobs on the machine's front. Janome has a knob which comes with different letters. Anytime you get that knob turned, you've changed the form of stitch (zig – zag, straight stitch and others). Beneath is another knob that changes the stitch's length.

These could be long stitches, tiny stitches, close together stitches and so on. This will be determined by that knob. There is a stitch guide which you will find on the right hand of these two. This will display the different stitch options of this machine. Again, if you want to select the particular stitch to be made use of, there is a knob on top which you will have to turn on.

Length adjustment of a sewing machine

On the machine's side, there is turning wheel. It is referred to as the hand wheel. It will be responsible for your wheel moving up and down. Most people including myself didn't actually know what this was called.

Using a sewing machine

This is a vital part of a sewing machine. Just pay attention to the details here and you will definitely get the whole idea that I am trying to pass across. There is the stitch lever (reverse). Anytime you plan sewing in reverse or backwards, just have it pulled down.

There is a dial which is close to the machine's top. It can be used in adjusting the stitch's width. This doesn't really matter when it comes to a straight stitch. However, for zig – zag stitch, it is going to determine whether the zig zag will be big and fat, narrow or even small.

How to sew

There is a knob on your machine's far side which can be used in adjusting the presser foot's tension. Most of the time, I usually leave it like that in my own case. Well, you know understand its functions.

Your machine has a metal part which is referred to as presser foot. Above it, is a lever which you can make use of in getting it lowered in order to sew. If you want to remove such fabric, get it raised.

There are some features which are fun to explore. For instance there is a tape which is built – in. As a matter of fact, I actually noticed this measuring tape on the machine of Carrie and had to check whether mine has it as well.

Are you aware that the machine's front part has a storage space? You will not be able to tell how vital this can be until you are sewing some materials.

Threading a sewing machine

How can this thing be threaded? This is very essential to your sewing exercise. Before this lesson will get started, you will have to practice this process for a minimum of about 10 times. I will not be able to show you how your machine can be threaded given that each machine seems to be different.

You will be shown how to do it by your manual. However, majority of sewing machines seem to be very similar. I will show you the way that Carrie's machine is being threaded.

For a start, the spindle is where the spool of thread will be put at the machine's top.

Ensure that the spool holder is in place in order so that your thread doesn't fly off. It is the plastic thing which is on the thread's left up there.

Now, grab the thread's ending and look for those nook and crannies where it can be pulled through. You can check your machine's guide in order to get some help on this.

How can I get my sewing machine threaded? Go down the grey part's right using your thread. Get it looped at the bottom and move up the left –

Sewing Machines

There is a small thread take-up lever that you will find at the top.

How a sewing machine can be used
You will be getting it threaded through some things. There is a small metal piece at your right that you need to see. It is below the machine's white part.

There is also another little metal piece. It is at the needle's top.

Understanding the parts of sewing machine.

Finally, get the needle threaded. If you practise this over and over again, you will see how it easy it can be to get it done even with your eyes shut down.

How bobbin can be threaded

Now you want to get your bobbin threaded. Before sewing, your bobbin needs to be winded. This will need to be done prior to getting your machine threaded for any project.

Below is a video showing how such process can be done.

You will need to take an empty bobbin cartridge as well as the particular color of thread that is needed. On the bobbin cartridge, you will find a very tiny hole that the thread will be able to pass through. Of course, your manual will be there to give you a guide on how this is done on your own machine. It is going to involve getting your thread put on the spindle. Get it wrapped around something such as this. You can see the silver button there. Just get it wrapped around it once.

The whole cartridge should be placed on this.

Continue hanging onto such thread's end even when bobbin cartridge seems to be on bobbin winder. The bobbin winder should be slide down to the right. Winding is now ready.

Continue hanging onto such thread. Also, get your foot pedal pushed down. Winding should start at this point. As it begins, get your scissors and then have the thread snipped which you are holding. Now, the bobbin should continue winding until when it gets full. Get it slided back to the left after which you can then have it removed.

For the bobbin to be inserted in the machine, the bobbin cover will need to be taken off. Now get your bobbin placed in its slot. This section is likely to appear different in your own machine. Once it is, don't forget to make use of your own manual.

It is through the manual that you will understand the direction which your bobbin spool will be turning to. It will be turning clockwise in the case of this machine.

Therefore, before I would get it put in, want my bobbin lined up.

Now, I will get my bobbin's small placed down into hole and have the thread pulled through the small slot. This is in order to have it secured into such place.

Give the thread's ending a small and gentle push. Your bobbin should turn in the indicated direction.

Now, get the machine threaded. With the use of the hand wheel, have the thread needle lowered down and then back once again. The bobbin thread will be caught and pulled up using the needle. Both threads should be pulled to the side with your bobbin case getting closed.

Now you are ready to sew.

How a computerized sewing machine is used

It is high time we switched over to my machine. Below are some screen shots of how it looks like. The reason why I want to show is that it is computerized. Do you have something that looks like this? If that's the case, then below is a walkthrough on how it can be effectively used.

One major way that computerized machines have proven to be different is how stitches are selected. There are various stitch options that you can choose from. All I have to do is press the button if I want any of the options.

After that, stitch length as well as width will be adjusted through having the adjust button touched.

There are also buttons for reversing, getting the needle pulled up as well as down. There is also a knot which looks fanciful.

Also, if I want the machine to be stitching very fast, there is a slide for this.

My machine comes with a needle threader that is automatic which can be very helpful.

Apart from these features, the others are similar to what I have explained to you earlier on.

One thing that you will need to also note is that your machine has seam guides. For instance, if you are told that 1/2inch should be sewed, you will want your fabric's edge to be lined up in way that it is parallel with such a guide. The more you sew, the more this is going to make sense.

Conclusion

Once you start to implement the steps outlined you will be able to use a sewing machine to sew beautiful garments and patterns. Good luck and enjoy!

Printed in the USA
CPSIA information can be obtained
at www.ICGtesting.com
LVHW081043111023
760801LV00024B/339